VETERANS DAY

HOLIDAYS

Lynda Sorensen

The Rourke Press, Inc.
Vero Beach, Florida 32964

Edited by Sandra A. Robinson

PHOTO CREDITS
© James P. Rowan: cover, pages 4, 17, 18; © Emil Punter/Photo
Vision: page 10; © Lynn M. Stone: title page, page 21; courtesy U.S.
Army Military History Institute: pages 7, 8; permission First Division
Museum at Cantigny (Wheaton, IL): pages 12-13, 15

Library of Congress Cataloging-in-Publication Data

Sorensen, Lynda, 1953-
    Veterans day / Lynda Sorensen.
    p. cm. — (Holidays)
    Includes index.
    ISBN 1-57103-070-0
    1. Veterans Day—Juvenile literature. I. Title.
II. Series: Sorensen, Lynda, 1953-.   Holidays.
D671.S67   1994
394.2'684—dc20   94-17721
                                                        CIP
Printed in the USA   AC

TABLE OF CONTENTS

VETERANS DAY

Veterans Day honors the men and women who have served in America's armed forces. The armed, or **military,** services are America's Air Force, Army, Navy, Coast Guard and Marines.

Veterans Day is a **national** holiday. It is celebrated on November 11. Canada honors its **veterans** on Remembrance Day, which is also on November 11.

Veterans Day is a **patriotic** holiday. The day gives all Americans a chance to say "thanks" to veterans for helping to keep America strong and free.

Veterans Day remembers the men and women who served in all branches of the armed services

ARMISTICE DAY

What we now call Veterans Day used to be known as Armistice Day.

Armistice Day celebrated the day the fighting in World War I ended — November 11, 1918.

Nearly 9 million soldiers from many nations died in World War I (1914-1918). One hundred and sixteen thousand were Americans. World War I was supposed to be "the war to end all wars."

No one knew then that an even more terrible war would follow — World War II (1939-1945).

World War I American soldiers in trenches await a German attack in France

ARMISTICE

World War I lasted for four long, bloody years. France, England, Russia and their **allies** fought against Germany and its allies. Canada joined the war against Germany in 1915. America entered the war against Germany in 1917.

Although World War I ended officially with the signing of a peace treaty in 1919, the fighting stopped in 1918 with a cease-fire, or **armistice.** The armistice began at 11 o'clock in the morning of the 11th day of the 11th month, 1918.

World War I officially ended with the signing of the Treaty of Versailles in May, 1919

TWO MINUTES OF SILENCE

After the armistice had been signed, Australian writer George Honey had an idea. He suggested that people worldwide spend two minutes of silence remembering the soldiers killed in action.

Honey's idea was very popular. Two minutes of silence became a Veterans Day tradition. Many Veterans Day ceremonies still include the two minutes of silence at 11 o'clock in the morning of the 11th day of the 11th month.

Many Veterans Day services still observe two minutes of silence at 11 a.m. on November 11

*Artist James Dietz captured some of the terrible combat of World War I
the First Division Museum at*

in this painting entitled, "I Have Assumed Command," on display at Cantigny, Wheaton, Illinois

RENAMING ARMISTICE DAY

The first Armistice Day holiday was held on November 11, 1919. It was celebrated in the United States every year until 1954.

By 1954 America had fought in World War II and the Korean War (1950-1953). **Congress** decided that America should have a day to honor all war veterans — living and dead. Congress renamed Armistice Day. November 11 became Veterans Day.

The "new" holiday honored the peace of 1918 and all the veterans of America's armed services.

14

James Dietz shows alert American foot soldiers during World War II action against the Germans in a painting on display at the First Division Museum at Cantigny, Wheaton, Illinois

TOMB OF THE UNKNOWNS

On November 11, 1921, an unidentified American soldier who had died in World War I was buried in the Tomb of the Unknown Soldier. Today this marble tomb at Arlington National Cemetery in Virginia is called the Tomb of the Unknowns. Unidentified soldiers from World War I, World War II, the Korean War and the Vietnam War are buried there.

Each Veterans Day a special ceremony honoring American soldiers killed in action is held at the Tomb of the Unknowns.

The remains of unidentified American soldiers from four wars are buried in the Tomb of the Unknowns

VIETNAM VETERANS MEMORIAL

The Vietnam Veterans Memorial lists the names of nearly 60,000 American soldiers who died in the Vietnam War (1965-1973).

Each Veterans Day a wreath is laid on the black granite memorial wall in Washington, D.C. The wreath is one way America honors and remembers veterans who died fighting the war in Vietnam.

A large bronze **sculpture** of three American soldiers is also part of the Vietnam Veterans Memorial (see cover of this book).

People walk slowly by the Vietnam Veterans Memorial in Washington, D.C.

19

VETERANS' ORGANIZATIONS

Veterans' organizations are groups of men and women who have been in the armed forces. They help organize and carry out ceremonies for Veterans Day and Memorial Day (May 30 or 31).

They help care for **disabled** veterans and the families of veterans who have died. Veterans' organizations also tell Congress and the public about veterans' needs, interests and concerns.

Two of the largest and oldest veterans' organizations are the American Legion and the Veterans of Foreign Wars.

The Veterans of Foreign Wars and other veterans' organizations are active in Veterans Day ceremonies

CELEBRATING VETERANS DAY

Some offices and most schools close on Veterans Day. Towns have parades and invite veterans to make speeches about the importance of serving America in the armed services.

Some schools invite veterans to share their experiences with students. Many veterans are a very real part of American wartime history. The lessons they teach are some of the most important the students will ever hear.

Glossary

allies (AH lies) — partners; in war, nations fighting on the same side

armistice (ARE muh stihss) — a temporary peace; an agreement between warring nations to stop fighting before a peace treaty is signed

Congress (KAHN gress) — in the United States, a group of lawmakers representing the states

disabled (dis A buld) — unable to perform certain tasks because of a permanent injury or illness; handicapped

military (MIL uh tar ee) — relating to a nation's armed services — its army, navy, air force, marines and coast guard

national (NAH shun ul) — of or relating to a nation

patriotic (pay tree AHT ihk) — referring to love of and loyalty to a country

sculpture (SKULPT chur) — a carving in stone, bronze or some other hard material

veteran (VEH ter in) — a former soldier; a man or a woman who served in the armed forces, for example, America's Air Force, Army, Navy, Coast Guard or Marines

INDEX